HOW GROOVY WAS YOUR GRAN?

Andrew Solway

Raintree

www.raintreepublishers.co.uk
Visit our website to find out more information about **Raintree** books.

To order:
☎ Phone 44 (0) 1865 888112
📄 Send a fax to 44 (0) 1865 314091
💻 Visit the Raintree bookshop at **www.raintreepublishers.co.uk** to browse our catalogue and order online.

First published in Great Britain by Raintree, Halley Court, Jordan Hill, Oxford OX2 8EJ, part of Pearson Education.

Raintree is a registered trademark of Pearson Education Ltd.

© Pearson Education Ltd 2008
First published in paperback in 2008
The moral right of the proprietor has been asserted.

Editorial: Louise Galpine, Harriet Milles, and Rachel Howells
Design: Richard Parker and Tinstar Design www.tinstar.co.uk
Illustrations: International Mapping
Picture Research: Ruth Blair
Production: Alison Parsons
Originated by Modern Age
Printed and bound in China by Leo Paper Group

13-digit ISBN 978 1 4062 0844 3 (hardback)
12 11 10 09 08
10 9 8 7 6 5 4 3 2 1

13-digit ISBN 978 1 4062 0852 8 (paperback)
12 11 10 09 08
10 9 8 7 6 5 4 3 2

British Library Cataloguing in Publication Data
Solway, Andrew
How groovy was your gran? - (Fusion history)
1. Nineteen fifties - Juvenile literature 2. Nineteen sixties - Juvenile literature 3. Great Britain - Social life and customs - 1945- - Juvenile literature
I. Title
941'.085
A full catalogue record for this book is available from the British Library

Acknowledgements
The publishers would like to thank the following for permission to reproduce photographs: Alamy pp. **8** (The Photolibrary Wales), **10** (Photofusion Picture Library), **13** (Popperfoto), **15** (Ben Molyneux), **21** (Photos 12); Corbis pp. **11**, **14**, **27**, **28** (Hulton-Deutsch Collection), **16** (BBC), **22** (Condé Nast Archive), **23** (Bettmann); Mary Evans Picture Library p. **9**; Photoshot/UPPA p. **7**; Rex Features pp. **17**, **19**, **5** (Frank Bell), **18**, **24** (Brian Moody), **25** (Brian Rasic); The Kobal Collection/Metro media p. **12**.

Cover photograph of model wearing lizard skin shoes reproduced with permission of Corbis/Conde Naste Archive.

Every effort has been made to contact copyright holders of any material reproduced in this book. Any omissions will be rectified in subsequent printings if notice is given to the publishers.

The publishers would like to thank Bill Mariott and Lynne Bold for their assistance with the preparation of this book.

Disclaimer
All the Internet addresses (URLs) given in this book were valid at the time of going to press. However, due to the dynamic nature of the Internet, some addresses may have changed, or sites may have changed or ceased to exist since publication. While the author and publishers regret any inconvenience this may cause readers, no responsibility for any such changes can be accepted by either the author or the publishers.

It is recommended that adults supervise children on the Internet.

Contents

Some words are printed in bold, **like this**. You can find out what they mean on page 30. You can also look in the box at the bottom of the page where they first appear.

Was your gran there?

Does your gran ride a big motorbike? Does your grandad wear flared velvet trousers? Probably not! But what about when they were young? What did they get up to then?

Your grandparents were probably teenagers in the 1950s or 1960s. Britain was not much fun in the early 1950s. The country was recovering from **World War II**. Wars are expensive, so Britain was poor. Food and clothes were **rationed**. Britain was short of houses to live in. Many houses had been bombed in the war.

By the 1960s, things had improved. People had more money. They had more free time. There were new houses being built. British music, fashion, and design were famous around the world.

So was your gran a "groovy chick"? Was granddad a "boss hipster"? Read on and find out about the 1950s and 1960s. Then ask your grandparents: What *did* you get up to?

The 1950s were not all gloomy. When Queen Elizabeth II was crowned in 1953, there were street parties like this one all over the country.

rationed   if something is rationed you are only allowed a certain amount of it

World War II   war fought from 1939 to 1945

New arrivals

Did your gran or grandad come to Britain from abroad? In 1948, the ship SS *Empire Windrush* arrived in London from the Caribbean. The people on board were **immigrants** from Jamaica and Trinidad. Many of them had been soldiers fighting for Britain in the war. They came to look for work.

More Caribbean people moved to Britain in the 1950s and 1960s. Other people arrived from India, Pakistan, and Bangladesh. All these places had been British **colonies**.

The SS Empire Windrush picked up people in Jamaica, and brought them to England.

- ← voyage of SS Windrush
- ⊛ capital city
- — modern day borders

CANADA

GREAT BRITAIN

London

FRANCE

UNITED STATES

ATLANTIC OCEAN

MEXICO

THE CARIBBEAN ISLANDS

AFRICA

JAMAICA ⊛ Kingston

Caribbean Sea

TRINIDAD

| 0 | 500 | 1,000 miles |
| 0 | 500 | 1,000 kilometres |

colony   place that is ruled by people from another country
culture   customs and traditions of a place or people
immigrant   someone from abroad who comes to live in a new country

Most of the passengers who came to England on the SS Empire Windrush were young men.

At first life was difficult for the new arrivals. There were plenty of jobs, but not enough places to live. Some British people became angry. They said that the immigrants were taking homes that British people needed.

Soon the immigrants built new lives for themselves. They joined in with life in Britain. They also brought some of their own music and **culture** to Britain.

Food, lovely food

Is your gran a good cook? In the 1950s, people had to be **inventive** about cooking. They had to try to make nice meals from very little food. This was because some food was still **rationed**.

Food rationing began during **World War II**. This was because Britain could no longer get the food it needed from abroad. Everyone was allowed only a certain amount of food each week.

In the 1950s you did not serve yourself in shops. You asked the shopkeeper for what you wanted.

inventive   to have good ideas about how to make things

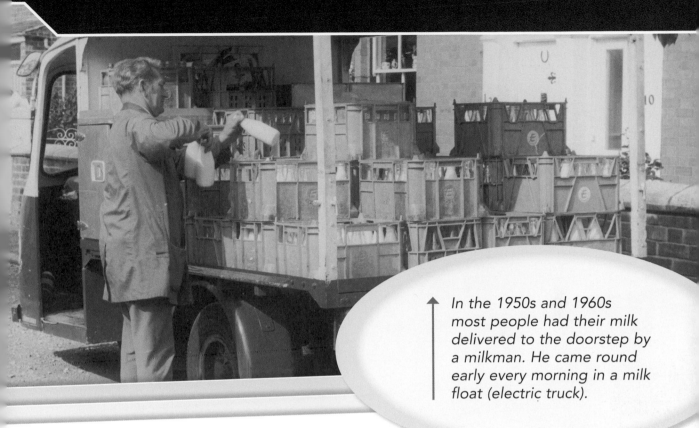

In the 1950s and 1960s most people had their milk delivered to the doorstep by a milkman. He came round early every morning in a milk float (electric truck).

In the 1950s most people went to small shops for their food. Meat came from the butcher's. Fruit and vegetables came from the greengrocer's. The grocer's shop sold most other kinds of food.

Less food was sold in packets. You could not pick what you wanted from the shelves. The shopkeeper cut and weighed out the amounts of each food that the customer wanted.

Food facts

In the early 1950s, rations for one person each week included:

- 1 fresh egg
- 50g (1.75 oz) butter
- 50g (1.75 oz) cheese.

You were also allowed 350g (12 oz) of sweets every month!

Building new homes

Where did your grandparents live when they were young? Did they live in an old **terraced** house, or a modern flat? Before **World War II**, millions of people lived in small, terraced houses. There was no bathroom. The toilet was usually outdoors.

Your grandparents might have lived in terraced houses like these in Manchester.

cooking range old-fashioned cooker that used coal rather than gas or electricity

terraced in a row, joined together

Prefabs

In the 1950s the government built small houses called prefabs. The word "prefab" is short for "pre-fabricated". This means that large parts of the houses were made in factories. Then they were put together on the building site. Prefabs were only meant to last a few years. However, some are still being used today, over 60 years later. You can see some prefabs below the flats in the photo.

In the 1950s, the government began building new houses and flats. They wanted to replace the old terraces. They planned new towns such as Milton Keynes and Telford. The new houses and flats had bathrooms, toilets, and gardens.

Inside, the homes had built-in kitchens instead of an old-style **cooking range.** They had central heating instead of coal fires. The new towns provided homes for millions of people. But many people did not like the new, "boxy" designs.

Rock 'n' roll

Was your grandad a **Teddy boy**? Was your gran a great little **jiver**? In the mid-1950s, a new kind of music came to Britain from the United States. It was called rock 'n' roll.

Most parents did not like the new music. They thought it was too wild and loud. But young people loved it. Stars such as Elvis Presley and Chuck Berry were world-famous.

Rock 'n' roll star Chuck Berry was a great showman. In this photo he is doing his famous "duck walk" on stage.

jive dance for couples in the 1950s
jukebox coin-operated machine that plays a choice of records
Teddy boy young man who wore a long jacket and tight "drainpipe" trousers

In the early days of rock 'n' roll, the most popular kind of dance was the jive. Jive dancers swing towards each other and away again, spin, and dance around each other. Sometimes the boy swings the girl into the air or over his shoulder.

New fashions and dancing came with rock 'n' roll. For the first time, young people dressed differently from their parents. Teddy boys wore long jackets, tight "drainpipe" trousers, and thick-soled shoes. Girls wore circle skirts and had big hairdos. They went to coffee bars and dance halls, where they danced the jive. They listened to music on the radio, or on **jukeboxes**. They played records on their record players. These were the first "teenagers".

Factories and offices

Do you know what job your grandad did? Did your gran work? In the 1950s and 1960s there were jobs for nearly everyone. There were far more jobs in factories than there are today. Now things that used to be made in British factories are made abroad.

These female workers are preparing medicines at a factory in Essex. It was easier for women to get jobs after World War II.

typewriter machine for printing letters on paper
typist person who has a job typing

Pounds, shillings, and pence

Before 1971 Britain's money was different. People used pounds (£), shillings (s), and old pence (d). One old penny was worth less than half a new penny. One shilling was 12 pence (5p in modern money). There were 20 shillings in a pound.

In those days, most big offices had a "typing pool". This was a big room full of **typists**, who worked on **typewriters**. They typed up letters and all kinds of other documents.

By the mid-1950s, food was not **rationed** any more. People were also earning more money. The average wage for men in 1954 was about £550 a year. This does not seem much in today's money. However, you could buy a house for £2,000 at that time.

Television and space

Your grandparents may have had a black-and-white TV set by 1953. In June, the Queen's **coronation** was shown live on television. Lots of people bought television sets especially to watch it. By the end of 1967, some people had colour TV.

These children are watching Andy Pandy, a children's television series which was first shown by the BBC (British Broadcasting Corporation) in 1950.

coronation when a queen or king is crowned
satellite any object that orbits (goes round) the Earth or another planet
Soviet Union state made of many countries in eastern Europe

In July 1969, the first ever Moon landing was shown live on TV. The colour pictures were beamed 250,000 miles across space.

There were many other new kinds of technology in the 1950s and 1960s:

- Plastics were used to make all kinds of things, from tabletops to stockings.

- Early computers were being used by scientists, banks, and big companies.

- Rockets launched **satellites** into space.

- In 1961 the **Soviet Union** sent the first astronaut into space. Only eight years later, the United States landed astronauts on the Moon.

Mods and rockers

Did your grandparents keep up with fashions? If they did, they would have been either mods or rockers in the early 1960s.

Mods mainly liked African-American music such as **Motown** and soul. They also liked Jamaican music such as **ska.** Boys wore parkas (hooded coats) and caps. Mod girls wore dresses and "go-go" boots (long leather boots). Mods often drove around on motor scooters.

Rockers liked rock music, especially Elvis Presley. Rockers wore leather jackets and jeans. They drove large motorbikes.

On summer weekends and bank holidays, mods and rockers headed for seaside towns such as Brighton and Hastings. They often got into fights with each other.

Let's Twist!

By the 1960s, young people were dancing alone rather than in couples. The biggest dance craze was the "Twist". The instructions for the Twist were: "Imagine you are stubbing out a cigarette with both feet while drying your back with a towel." Other popular dances included the "Madison", the "Mashed Potato", and the "Pony".

Motown   type of soulful pop music from the United States
ska   type of Jamaican music from the early 1960s

This photograph shows young mods with their motor scooters. Scooters were popular because young people were allowed to drive them when they were 16 years old.

19

Beat music

Did your gran ever go to a Beatles concert? In 1962, the Beatles released their first single, *Love Me Do*. By the end of 1963 they were the most popular band in Britain. By 1964 they were also a hit in the United States. Other British bands, such as The Who and the Rolling Stones, also had hits in the United States.

This photo shows the Beatles performing in 1964. They are, from left to right, Paul McCartney, George Harrison, Ringo Starr (on drums), and John Lennon.

Before the Beatles, teenagers listened mostly to American music. But the Beatles changed all that. Their tour of the United States in 1964 was a huge success. Everywhere the Beatles went, there were crowds of screaming fans. For the first time, Britain was setting new trends in music.

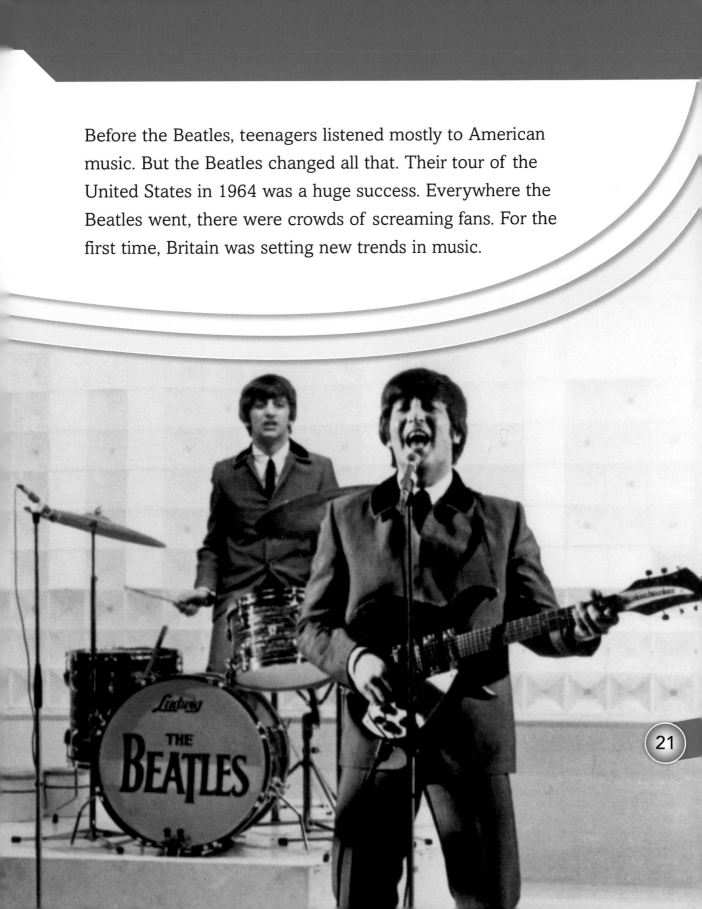

Swinging Britain

Were your grandparents trendy (fashionable) in the mid-1960s? At this time, Britain was "swinging" (exciting). 1960s teenagers could earn more money than young people in the 1950s. They could afford luxuries, such as records and fashionable clothes.

At this time, Britain became famous for its fashion and design. Britain led the world in new designs for everything from furniture to record covers. The original "Mini" was the most fashionable car of the time.

British dress designers produced world-famous fashions, such as the miniskirt.

This photo shows England captain Bobby Moore holding up the World Cup trophy. England beat Germany 4-2.

In 1966, the football World Cup was held in Britain. Even people who were not football fans became interested for a short time. England won the World Cup after a thrilling final match against Germany.

Peace and love

Was your gran a hippy? If so, she may have been at the first free pop festival in Hyde Park, London, in June 1968. The bands that played there included Pink Floyd and Tyrannosaurus Rex. Most people at the festival were hippies.

Hippies believed in peace and love. They thought that there were too many wars. They believed that people cared too much about making money. Hippy men and women had long hair. They wore bright clothes, bead necklaces, and sandals. They often wore flowers in their hair. This time was known as the "flower-power era".

The Rolling Stones performed at this free concert in Hyde Park, London, in 1969.

nuclear immensely powerful force

The bright colours and swirling patterns of this record cover were called "psychedelic art". Cream were one of the most popular rock groups of the hippy era.

Most hippies took drugs that gave them strange, "psychedelic" visions. "Psychedelic" means dream-like. Hippy music was often "psychedelic" too.

Nuclear protests

In the 1960s the United States and the **Soviet Union** both built up large stocks of **nuclear** weapons. Hippies and many other young people were very worried by this. If either country used their nuclear weapons for war, it would affect the whole world.

The end of an era

Your grandparents probably saw a lot of changes between 1948 and 1968. In 1948 people were struggling to find homes and feed their families. By the end of the 1960s people had more money. They wanted more fun.

One way they had fun was to go on holiday. In the 1960s, the most popular places for holidays were holiday camps. These were seaside places with specially built holiday cabins, swimming pools, and fun things to do. People could go ballroom dancing, play table tennis or snooker, and enter a "knobbly knees" contest, all in one day! There were also clubs for children, and help with childcare.

Many people could afford to go abroad for the first time. Jet airliners flew regularly to places around the world. Travel companies offered "package holidays" to foreign countries. The "package" included the air flight, a place to stay, meals, and often trips to places of interest.

This photograph shows the very first passengers boarding the very first passenger jet airliner flight in 1952. By the 1960s jets had made flying cheap and fast.

Cool talk

If your gran and grandad were really groovy in the 1950s and 1960s, they would have used some of the words in the box below:

Hip words

Slang	Meaning
boss	really good
bread	money
bug	bother
cat	person
chick	girl
crash pad	place to sleep
dig the scene	enjoy what's going on
dullsville	boring
frosted	angry
go ape	get really angry
groovy	excellent
hip	cool, in the know
swinging	exciting or up-to-date
threads	clothes

Fashionable young people, like these from 1955, often met in coffee bars to relax and talk together.

Timeline

1948

SS *Empire Windrush* brings 500 people to Britain from the Caribbean.

National Health Service (NHS) offers free health care to everyone for the first time.

1950

Mass production of computers begins.

1952

London smog (a mixture of smoke and fog) kills over 2,000 people.

First singles charts. A song called *Here in My Heart* by Al Martino was Number 1.

1953

Coronation of Queen Elizabeth II.

1954

Roger Bannister is the first person to run one mile (1.6 kilometres) in less than 4 minutes.

1956

The first large **nuclear** power station in the world is opened at Calder Hill, Cumbria. It makes electricity using nuclear power.

End of food **rationing**.

1957

Russians launch Sputnik **satellite**.

1959

The Morris Mini car first goes on sale.

The microchip is invented.

1961

Russian Yuri Gagarin becomes the first human in space.

1962

First Beatles single, *Love Me Do*, is released.

1963

US President John F. Kennedy is assassinated (killed). *Doctor Who* is first shown on TV.

1964

The Beatles tour the United States.

Miniskirts become fashionable.

1966

England wins the football World Cup.

1968

Crowds demonstrate in London against US military action in Vietnam.

Martin Luther King is assassinated.

1969

US astronaut Neil Armstrong is first human on the Moon.

Glossary

colony place that is ruled by people from another country

cooking range old-fashioned cooker that used coal rather than gas or electricity

coronation when a queen or king is crowned. Queen Elizabeth II's coronation was in 1953.

culture customs and traditions of a place or people. This could include music, literature, religion, or food.

immigrant someone from abroad who comes to live in a new country. In the 1950s and 1960s immigrants came to the UK from the Caribbean and South Asia.

inventive to have good ideas about how to make things

jive dance for couples that arrived in Britain from the US in the 1950s. Men swung their partners round and sometimes lifted them into the air.

jukebox coin-operated machine that plays a choice of records. Jukeboxes were first invented in America, and could be found in bars and cafes.

Motown type of soulful pop music from the United States. Stars such as Diana Ross, Marvin Gaye, and the Jackson Five were Motown musicians.

nuclear immensely powerful force

rationed if something is rationed you are only allowed a certain amount of it. Food and clothes were rationed in Britain during World War II and the 1950s.

satellite any object that orbits (goes round) the Earth or another planet. In the 1960s the first artificial satellites were launched into orbit.

ska type of Jamaican music from the early 1960s. Reggae music developed from ska.

Soviet Union state made of many countries in eastern Europe. This existed from 1922 until 1991.

Teddy boy young man who wore a long jacket and tight "drainpipe" trousers. Teddy boys were a teenage fashion from the mid-1950s.

terraced in a row, joined together. In the 1950s the government wanted to get rid of old terraced houses, but many still exist today.

typewriter machine for printing letters on paper. Businesses relied on typewriters until personal computers were developed in the 1980s.

typist person who has a job typing

World War II war fought from 1939 to 1945. Britain and France declared war on Germany in 1939.

Want to know more?

Books to read

Look at Life in the Sixties, R. G. Grant (Raintree, 2000)

Picture History of the 20th Century: The 1950s, Richard Tames
      (Sea to Sea Publications, 2005)

Picture History of the 20th Century: The 1960s, Tim Healey
      (Sea to Sea Publications, 2005)

Websites

www.bbc.co.uk/cult/ilove/years/60sindex.shtml
You can find timelines, television, trivia, and lots of other information about
the 1960s on this BBC website.

www.museumoflondon.org.uk/archive/exhibits/festival/index.htm
The Museum of London's website has information about the Festival of
Britain in 1951. It includes the memories of many people who were there.

www.vam.ac.uk/collections/fashion/1960s/index.html
The Victoria and Albert Museum website has information about 1960s fashions.

Learn all about World
War II and evacuee
children in **When Can I
Come Home?**

Read about one of
history's most famous
round-the-world voyages
in **Captain's Log**.

Index